BOUNDARIES

PARTICIPANT'S GUIDE

Books by Drs. Henry Cloud and John Townsend

Boundaries
Boundaries Workbook
Boundaries audio
Boundaries video curriculum
Boundaries in Dating
Boundaries in Dating Workbook
Boundaries in Dating audio
Boundaries in Dating curriculum
Boundaries in Marriage
Boundaries in Marriage Workbook
Boundaries in Marriage audio
Boundaries with Kids
Boundaries with Kids Workbook
Boundaries with Kids audio
Changes That Heal (Cloud)
Changes That Heal Workbook (Cloud)
Changes That Heal audio (Cloud)
Hiding from Love (Townsend)
How People Grow
How People Grow audio
The Mom Factor
The Mom Factor Workbook
The Mom Factor audio
Raising Great Kids
Raising Great Kids for Parents of Preschoolers curriculum
Raising Great Kids Workbook for Parents of Preschoolers
Raising Great Kids Workbook for Parents of School-Age Children
Raising Great Kids Workbook for Parents of Teenagers
Raising Great Kids audio
Safe People
Safe People Workbook
Safe People audio
Twelve "Christian" Beliefs That Can Drive You Crazy

BOUNDARIES

When to Say YES
When to Say NO
To Take Control of Your Life

Dr. Henry Cloud
Dr. John Townsend

with Lisa Guest

ZONDERVAN™

GRAND RAPIDS, MICHIGAN 49530

ZONDERVAN™

Boundaries Participant's Guide
Copyright © 1999 by Henry Cloud and John Townsend

Requests for information should be addressed to:

Zondervan, *Grand Rapids, Michigan 49530*

ISBN 0-310-22453-5

Published in association with Yates & Yates, LLP, Literary Agent, Orange, CA..

Interior design by Sherri L. Hoffman

Printed in the United States of America

05 06 07 /❖DC/ 19 18 17 16 15

Contents

Preface

Many sincere, dedicated believers struggle with tremendous confusion about when it is biblically appropriate to set limits. Attempting to serve the Lord and die to self as Jesus modeled, these Christians try hard, are nice, and help others out—but their unproductive energy, fearful niceness, and overresponsibility point to the core problem: they suffer from severe difficulties in taking ownership of their life.

When confronted about their lack of boundaries, these people raise good questions:

- Can I set limits and still be a loving person?
- What are legitimate boundaries?
- What if someone is upset or hurt by my boundaries?
- How do I answer someone who wants my time, love, energy, or money?
- Why do I feel guilty or afraid when I consider setting boundaries?
- How do boundaries relate to submission?
- Aren't boundaries selfish?
- Is it difficult for me to hear no from other people?
- Do I tend to want to control other people when I don't get what I want?

This video series presents a biblical view of boundaries: what they are, what they protect, how they are developed, how they are injured, how to repair them, and how to use them. Our goal is to help you use biblical boundaries appropriately to achieve the relationships and purposes that God intends for you as his child. We aim to help you see the deeply biblical nature of boundaries as they operate in the character of God, his universe, and his people.

Henry Cloud, Ph.D.
John Townsend, Ph.D.

What Is a Boundary?

OVERVIEW

In this session you will

- Define what boundaries are—and why they are important

- Identify some examples of boundaries

- Find out what we are responsible for within our boundaries

- Learn that the concept of boundaries comes from the nature of God himself

- Discover how boundaries result in freedom, which leads to love

VIDEO SEGMENT
Sherrie Without Boundaries

- Sherrie is trying to do a good job with her marriage, her children, her job, her relationships, and her Lord. Yet it's obvious that something isn't right. Life isn't working.

- Sherrie isn't able to draw and maintain boundaries around what is hers, boundaries that would help keep out what isn't hers.

- In the physical world, boundaries are easy to see, and they give the message: THIS IS WHERE MY PROPERTY BEGINS. The owner of the property is legally responsible for what happens on his or her property. Nonowners are not responsible for the property.

- Just as homeowners set physical property lines around their property, we need to set mental, physical, emotional, and spiritual boundaries for our lives to help us distinguish what is our responsibility and what isn't.

- A variety of things, including past hurts, poor models, and misunderstood Christian teachings, cause weak boundaries or boundaries that don't exist at all.

- Boundaries define *what is me* and *what is not me*. A boundary shows where each individual ends and someone else begins, leading each person to a sense of ownership and responsibility. Boundaries also protect us from the bad.

LET'S TALK

Examples of Boundaries and the Responsibilities That Come with Them

Directions

1. The leader will split the large group into seven small groups and assign each group a cluster from one of the lists found on pages 12–13.

2. If your group is assigned some examples of boundaries, talk about why each is considered a boundary and what people can do to keep that particular boundary strong.

3. If your group is assigned some of the responsibilities that come with boundaries, talk about what being responsible for each of these areas involves or (perhaps an easier question to answer) what irresponsibility in each area looks like.

4. When you come back together as a large group, a spokesperson from each small group will share your group's ideas with the others.

5. You'll also notice some "Boundary Building" questions at the end of each page. These important questions—intended for later—can help you build healthy boundaries for yourself.

6. You will have 8 minutes to complete this exercise.

Examples of Boundaries

Cluster A: *Skin* (What good does skin keep in and what bad does it keep out?); *words* (especially the word *no*)

Cluster B: *Truth* (about God and about who you are); *time* (as in "time away from")

Cluster C: *Geographical distance* (removing yourself from a situation); *emotional distance* (guarding your heart)

Cluster D: *Other people* (How can other people help you set and keep boundaries?); *consequences* (Why are consequences necessary to strong boundaries?)

BOUNDARY BUILDING ———————

1. Think of a time when you stuck by your boundary in a particular area and people honored it. (What were the circumstances? Why were you able to maintain your boundary? How did people respond? What did you learn from this experience?) Consider what hinders you from keeping each boundary strong. (Look back at a time when someone did not honor a boundary you set and try to identify why that happened.)
2. Now consider the list of boundaries from another perspective. Which boundaries, when set by other people, do *you* need to do a better job of honoring? Why might you have a hard time honoring people's boundaries, especially certain ones? What will you do to be more respectful of the boundaries of the people in your life?

Responsibilities That Come with Boundaries

Cluster E: *Feelings, attitudes/beliefs, desires*

Cluster F: *Behaviors, choices, values, thoughts*

Cluster G: *Limits, talents, love/trust*

BOUNDARY BUILDING —————

1. What do you tend to do with your *feelings* (especially anger)—ignore them or let them be in charge? Why do you think you respond in the way you do?

2. Which *attitudes and beliefs* do you hold that are causing you to make poor choices or experience pain? What will you do to get those attitudes and beliefs in line with God's truth?

3. Paul says, "A man reaps what he sows" (Gal. 6:7). When has someone interrupted the law of sowing and reaping in your life and protected you from *consequences* that could have been good teachers? What happened?

4. What *choices* in your life have you failed to take responsibility for? Whom are you blaming for what circumstances of your life?

5. When have you been caught up in *valuing* the approval of people rather than the approval of God (John 12:43)? What lesson did you learn from that experience or from seeing someone else caught in that trap?

Continued on next page . . .

Boundary Building—continued from previous page

6. Where in your life today would you do well to *limit* your exposure to someone? What is keeping you from doing so? What destructive desires do you need to learn to say no to? What good desires do you need to learn to say no to because the timing isn't right?

7. What *talents*, gifts, and abilities are you currently exercising? What talent, gift, or ability are you afraid to exercise? What step will you take to overcome that fear?

8. Name one area of your life in which you would do well to *think* through some issues for yourself. What are you doing to grow in your knowledge of God and his Word? Whom are you expecting to be able to read your mind? To whom are you afraid to communicate your thoughts? What do you think keeps you from doing so?

9. When have you experienced the fulfillment of a God-given *desire?* Be specific about the circumstances and your feelings. What desires are you currently pursuing that your heavenly Father, wise parent that he is, is probably not interested in giving you?

10. How healthy is the inflow of *love* in your life? What healthy, godly relationships nurture you? How healthy is the outflow of love in your life? Where are you giving to others the kind of unconditional love God has given you?

MORE ON BOUNDARIES

- Boundaries help us distinguish our property so that we can
  _____ _____ _____ _____—and we
  are responsible for taking care of it. We need to keep things
  that will _____us inside our fences and keep
  things that will _____ us outside. In short,
  boundaries help us keep the _____ in and the
  _____ out. But these fences need to have gates so
  that we can let good in and let out any bad.

- This concept of boundaries comes from the very _____
  of God. God defines himself as a distinct being _____
  from his creation and from us. He has boundaries within the
  _____. The Father, the Son, and the Spirit are
  one, but at the same time they are distinct persons with
  their own boundaries.

- God also _____ what he will allow in his yard. He
  confronts sin and allows consequences for behavior. He
  guards his house and will not allow evil things to go on there.
  He invites people in who will love him, and he lets his love
  flow outward to them at the same time. Created _____
  _____ _____, we have personal responsibili-
  ties within limits, within boundaries that we set and maintain.

ON YOUR OWN
Responsible To *and Responsible* For

Directions

1. We've recognized that the concept of boundaries comes from the very nature of God. Now let's take a few minutes to look at what his Word teaches us. On your own, take some time to work through the Bible study you see in front of you.

2. After 8 minutes, you will pair up with the person next to you and talk about what you have learned from Galatians 6:1–5. Spend 5 minutes sharing what this passage helped you understand about boundaries and what you learned about how you deal with boulders and knapsacks.

Key to understanding and building healthy boundaries is realizing that we are responsible *to* others and *for* ourselves. Read Galatians 6:1–5.

1. What does Galatians 6:2 teach about responsibility to others? According to this verse, what is our responsibility to one another?

2. When has someone in your life followed Christ's example of sacrificial love and denied him/herself in order to do for you what you could not do for yourself?

3. When have you followed Christ's example of sacrificial love and denied yourself in order to do for others what they could not do for themselves?

4. Now look at Galatians 6:5. What does this verse teach about being responsible for ourselves?

The Greek words for *burden* and *load* give important insight into these two verses from Galatians. The Greek word for *burden* means "excess burdens," or boulders that we need help carrying. The Greek word for *load* means "cargo" or "the burden of daily toil." A load is like a knapsack. A knapsack is possible to carry, and we are expected to carry our own. In the same way, we are expected to deal with our own feelings, attitudes, and behaviors, as well as the responsibilities God has given us, even though it takes effort.

BOUNDARY BUILDING ⎯⎯⎯⎯

1. When have you or in what cases are you today acting as if your "boulders" are your daily load and refusing help?

2. When have you or in what cases are you today acting as if the "burden of daily toil" is a boulder you shouldn't have to carry?

3. What have these two questions helped you see about yourself—and what will you do with what you have learned?

VIDEO SEGMENT
Wrapping It Up

- Made in the image of God, we were created to take responsibility for certain tasks. Part of taking responsibility, or ownership, is knowing what is our job and what isn't. It takes wisdom to know what we should be doing and what we shouldn't.

- Knowing what we are to own and take responsibility for gives us freedom. If each of us knows where our yard begins and ends, we are free to do with it what we like.

- Boundaries do more than just allow us to care for ourselves. They also help us care for others in a healthy, Christlike way.

- Maintaining boundaries—or, put differently, taking responsibility for our life—opens up many different options. Realizing that we don't need to be limited by circumstances, other people, or the dictates of an internal critical voice, we can take greater control of our time, energy, and resources and experience the freedom of doing whatever we want and serving others in the ways we choose.

- The freedom that comes with knowing our own boundaries leads to love because love requires freedom. If we feel free to say no, then when we *choose* to give, we are giving out of love, and our service is truly Christlike.

- We need to take responsibility for our feelings, attitudes, beliefs, behaviors, choices, thoughts, values, limits, talents, desires, and love.

SUGGESTED READING ───────

For more thoughts on this session's topic, read chapters 1 and 2 in *Boundaries*: "A Day in a Boundaryless Life" and "What Does a Boundary Look Like?" For a more thorough self-evaluation, look at chapter 1 in the *Boundaries Workbook.*

Understanding Boundaries

OVERVIEW

In this session you will

- Identify specific struggles in establishing and enforcing boundaries

- Determine how boundary problems develop and how they are injured

BOUNDARY PROBLEMS

- _____ say yes to bad things because they
  haven't learned how to say no or even that it's okay to say no
  to the bad. Their weak boundaries let everything in.

- _____ say no to the good. They aren't able to
  ask for help; their boundaries keep people—and often even
  God—out. Needs, problems, and legitimate wants seem
  bad and destructive.

- _____ hear no as simply a challenge to change
  the other person's mind. Controllers can't respect other
  people's limits. Aggression and manipulation are two of the
  controller's main tools.

- _____ neglect the responsibilities of love by not
  responding to other people's needs. Critical or self-
  absorbed, nonresponsives ignore the needs of others.

- Another boundary issue involves the distinction between
  _____ and _____ boundaries. A prob-
  lem can arise because often people are good at one and not
  at the other. _____ _____ refers to
  a person's ability to complete a task, project, or job. It has to
  do with performance, discipline, initiative, and planning.
  _____ _____ refers to the ability
  to speak truth to others with whom we are in relationship.

LET'S TALK
Diagnosing Boundary Problems

Directions

1. The leader will divide you into six groups and assign each group a different one of the six scenarios found on the next few pages.

2. Once your group has been assigned a scenario, read through it. Then diagnose the boundary problem—compliant, avoidant, controller, nonresponsive, or a combination of these categories—exhibited by the person whose name appears in boldface type. Once you've made the diagnosis, discuss the questions you find listed under the scenario you read.

3. When you are called back together as a large group, a spokesperson from your group will read the group's scenario and share your group's ideas.

4. You will have 15 minutes to complete this exercise.

Scenario #1

Marti had begun to see a pattern in her life. In her words, "When someone needs four hours with me, I can't say no. But when *I* need someone for ten minutes, I can't ask for it. Isn't there a transistor in my head I can replace?"

Diagnosis: _____

- When is Marti compliant? When is she avoidant?
- Why would this cycle be draining?
- What problems might being a compliant avoidant cause in marriage? parenting? the workplace? relationships?
- What might be some other symptoms of a compliant avoidant?

Scenario #2

Brenda and **Mike** were talking in their bedroom after putting the kids to bed. Brenda began to unburden her fears about childrearing and her feelings of inadequacy at work. Without warning, Mike turned to her and said, "If you don't like the way you feel, change your feelings. Life's tough. So just . . . just handle it, Brenda."

Diagnosis: _____

- What is the difference between being responsible *for* another person and responsible *to* another person? Which is healthy? Why?
- Explain why nonresponsiveness is often expressed with criticism and has its roots in narcissism.
- What problems might Mike's nonresponsiveness cause in his marriage? his parenting? the workplace?
- What might be some other symptoms of a nonresponsive person?

Scenario #3

Robert was the only boy in his family, the youngest of four children. His sisters were three to seven years older than he was. Until he was in the sixth grade, they were bigger and stronger, and they would take advantage of their size and strength and beat him until he was bruised. His parents said, "Boys don't hit girls. It's bad manners." He was triple teamed, but was told that fighting back—protecting himself—was bad manners.

Diagnosis: _____

- What were Robert's parents teaching him about boundaries? (What did your parents teach you by their words and actions?)
- Why do some people say yes to bad things?
- What problems might Robert's compliance cause in his marriage? his parenting? the workplace?
- What might be some other symptoms of compliance?

Scenario #4

"What do you mean, you're quitting? You can't leave now!" **Steve** looked at Frank, his administrative assistant for several years. Frank had given his all, even spending unpaid time at the office on projects and switching his vacation schedule twice at Steve's insistence. The final straw came when Steve began calling Frank at home almost every day during dinnertime. Several times Frank had tried to talk with Steve about the time violations, but Steve never really understood. After all, he needed Frank: Frank made him look successful.

Diagnosis: _____

- What responsibility is Steve avoiding?
- How can a controller use aggression? manipulation?
- What problems might Steve's control cause in his marriage? his parenting? the workplace? his relationships?
- What might be some other symptoms of a controller?

Scenario #5

Tonight the five couples who had been meeting as a Bible study for six months suddenly became more intimate. The sharing went beyond the usual "please pray for Aunt Sarah" requests to the real struggles in their lives. When people asked their hostess, **Rachel**, to share, she cleared her throat and finally spoke: "After hearing all the other problems, the Lord seems to be saying that my issues are nothing compared to what you all deal with. So . . . who'd like dessert?"

Diagnosis: _____

- What has Rachel learned about boundaries? What has she learned about her problems and probably even her God-given needs?
- What problems arise when boundaries function more like walls than fences?
- What problems might Rachel's avoidance cause in her marriage? her parenting? the workplace? her relationships? her relationship with God?
- What might be some other symptoms of avoidance?

Scenario #6

Brad hung up the phone after talking to **Brenda**, his mom. Brad and his wife, Allison, had made plans for a much-needed getaway as a couple, but the date happened to fall on Brenda's birthday. When Brenda heard about the plans, she called Brad and complained to him about how selfish he was being and how lonely he was making her. When he tried to explain that their plans weren't directed against her and that he and Allison really needed the break, Brenda refused to listen to Brad's needs and concerns for his marriage. The couple scuttled their plans and resignedly prepared for the trip to Mom's.

Diagnosis: _____

- How is Brenda controlling? How is she nonresponsive at the same time?
- Why would a controlling nonresponsive be attracted to a compliant avoidant?
- What problems might being a controlling nonresponsive cause in her marriage? her parenting? the workplace? her relationships?
- What might be some other symptoms of a controlling non-responsive?

BOUNDARY BUILDING ─────────────

1. In which quadrant of the "Summary of Boundary Problems" chart (see below) do you see yourself? (You may find yourself in more than one!) In which quadrants would you categorize the people with whom you are struggling today?

SUMMARY OF BOUNDARY PROBLEMS

	CAN'T SAY	CAN'T HEAR
NO	The Compliant feels guilty and/or controlled by others; can't set boundaries	The Controller aggressively or manipulatively violates boundaries of others
YES	The Nonresponsive sets boundaries against responsibility to love	The Avoidant sets boundaries against receiving care from others

2. Do you have good functional boundaries but poor relational boundaries? Or do you have good relational boundaries but poor functional boundaries? Why do you think your boundary strengths and weaknesses are what they are?

A HANDFUL OF FACTS

- Boundaries aren't _____; they're _____.

- The Scriptures advise parents to "_____ a child in the way he _____ go, and when he is old he will not turn from it" (Prov. 22:6).

- Boundaries develop in distinct _____.

- Foundational to healthy boundary development are _____ _____ relationships with _____ and _____ _____.

- We human beings are built for _____ and _____ to one another.

VIDEO SEGMENT
Boundary Development and Obstacles to It

- Boundaries develop as a normal part of our interaction with our families.

- The first developmental task of infants is to bond with their mom and dad. They need to learn that they are welcome and safe in the world.

- Healthy bonding leads to healthy separation and individualism. The baby's need for autonomy, or independence, starts to emerge.

- Hatching, practicing, and rapprochement are three additional phases critical to the development of healthy boundaries.

- Two additional periods later in life also focus on boundaries. The first is adolescence. The adolescent years are in some ways similar to the first few years of life. They involve more mature issues, such as sexuality, gender identity, competition, and adult identity, but the same issues of knowing when to say yes and no and to whom are central during this confusing time.

- The second period is young adulthood, the time when children leave home or college and start a career or get married. Young adults suffer a loss of structure during this period and experience new demands of intimacy and commitment. This can be an intense time of learning more about setting good boundaries.

- The process of healthy boundary development can be interrupted by a variety of things—withdrawal of love when boundaries are exercised, hostility against boundaries, overcontrol, a lack of limits, inconsistent limits, trauma (or abuse), character traits, and sinfulness.

ON YOUR OWN
A Biblical View of Healthy Boundary Development

Directions

1. Take about 8 minutes to read the verses and answer the questions you find in this Bible study.

2. If you have time now, also consider the "Boundary Building" questions. If you run out of time, plan to look at them later.

Scripture offers great insight into what needs to happen in each phase of development and why each of these phases is crucial to the establishment of healthy boundaries.

Bonding or connecting with their parents gives infants a sense of safety and security.

1. In Genesis 2:18, what observation about human beings does God make?

2. What phrases from Ephesians 3:17 and Colossians 2:7 refer to this kind of emotional object constancy?

Separation refers to a child's needs to perceive of him- or herself as distinct from Mother, a "not me" experience. **Individuation**

describes the identity children develop while separating from Mother, a "me" experience. You can't have a "me" until you have a "not me." An individual must first determine who he or she *isn't* before discovering the true authentic aspects of his or her God-given identity.

> 3. Look at young Jesus in Luke 2:41–49. What evidence do you see here of separation? What evidence do you see of individuation?

Hatching occurs between five and ten months of age as infants move from "Mommy and me are the same" to "Mommy and me aren't the same." This period is a time of exploration, of touching, of tasting and feeling new things. Though children in this phase are still dependent on Mother, they aren't wrapped up in closeness with her. The months of nurturing have paid off—the child feels safe enough to start taking risks.

Practicing children are those who are trying to leave Mother behind. Their newfound ability to walk opens up a sense of omnipotence. What practicing infants need most from parents is a responsive delight in their delight, exhilaration at their exhilaration, and some safe limits to their practice. In the practicing phase, children learn that aggressiveness and taking initiative are good. Parents need to firmly and consistently set realistic boundaries without spoiling their child's enthusiasm.

Rapprochement, which occurs from around eighteen months to three years, is that phase when the grandiosity of the past few months slowly gives way to the realization that "I can't do everything I want." This phase is a return to connection with Mother, but this time the child brings a more separate self—as well as obnoxious, oppositional, temperamental, and downright angry behaviors—into the relationship. Children at this age become "no" addicts, refusing not only vegetables and nap time but also Popsicles and favorite toys. In this stage, parents need to encourage their child's own boundaries as well as help the child learn to respect others' boundaries.

4. In Matthew 5:37, Jesus calls us to let our yes be yes and our no be no. Why and when is it important for our children to be able to say no?

5. What does the warning of Proverbs 19:18 say about the importance of helping children learn to accept limits when they encounter a no?

BOUNDARY BUILDING ───────────

1. What attitude toward boundaries was modeled in the home in which you grew up?

2. How have your boundaries been injured? See the notes for the video "Boundary Development and Obstacles to It" for a list of things that can interrupt healthy boundary development.

SUGGESTED READING ──────────

For more thoughts on this session's topic, read chapters 3 and 4 in *Boundaries*: "Boundary Problems" and "How Boundaries Are Developed." For a more thorough self-evaluation, look at chapter 2 in the *Boundaries Workbook.*

The Laws of Boundaries, Part I

OVERVIEW

In this session you will

- Discover what the Bible says about how boundaries should operate in our lives

- Learn how boundaries can be developed all through our lives

VIDEO SEGMENT
Lessons in the Laws of Boundaries

- People raised in families where God's ways of boundaries are not practiced never know the principles that could have helped them operate in accord with reality instead of against it.

- The reality God has established is an orderly one based on knowable laws and principles. These spiritual realities are as real as gravity.

- Law #1 is the Law of Sowing and Reaping. This law of cause and effect is a basic law of life. When God tells us in Galatians 6:7–8 that we will reap what we sow, he is not punishing us; he's telling us how things really are.

- Law #2 is the Law of Responsibility, which includes loving others (Gal. 5:13–14; John 15:12). In fact, anytime you are not loving others, you are not taking full responsibility for yourself; you have disowned your heart. We are to *love* one another, not *be* one another. You are responsible for *yourself*. I am responsible for *myself* (Phil. 2:12–13).

LET'S TALK
Lessons in the Laws of Boundaries

Directions

1. Break into eight groups.

2. Each group will be assigned one question about Law #1 or Law #2 for discussion. When we come back together, a spokesperson from each group will share your group's ideas with the large group.

3. You will have 5 minutes to complete this exercise.

Law #1: The Law of Sowing and Reaping

1. What are some effects (the reaping) of certain everyday behaviors (the sowing)? Consider negatives (overeating, over-spending, selfishness, ignoring God's commandments, etc.) as well as positives (eating right, exercising regularly, budgeting wisely, etc.). Be sure to discuss the consequences (reaping) of enforcing or failing to enforce boundaries (sowing).

2. Give three examples of how or when parents interrupt the Law of Sowing and Reaping (Gal. 6:7–8) in their children's lives. What, for instance, has happened to the person who says, "I can't discipline my spending because I was never taught to save"?

3. We call a person who continually rescues or enables another person to be an irresponsible "codependent." What are some reasons why it is hard for codependent people to allow others to suffer consequences?

4. Why are consequences more effective teachers than confrontations?

BOUNDARY BUILDING ————

1. Give an example of positive and negative sowing in your life. In each case, what did you reap? What are you sowing now?

2. When have consequences for your actions prompted you to make some changes?

3. Where do you need to stop interrupting the law of sowing and reaping in someone's life?

Law #2: The Law of Responsibility

1. What would you say to someone who asked, "Create my own boundaries? Isn't that awfully selfish?"

2. Taking responsibility for one's life includes loving others (John 15:12). What does it mean that we are to *love* one another, not *be* one another?

3. Read Philippians 2:12–13. Explain the difference between being responsible *to* and being responsible *for*.

4. One aspect of being responsible *to* someone is setting limits on that person's destructive and irresponsible behavior. Why would rescuing that person from the consequences of his or her destructive behavior be irresponsible?

BOUNDARY BUILDING —————

1. What are you doing to take responsibility for your personal and spiritual growth?

2. Where are you trying to take responsibility for someone else's personal and spiritual growth?

3. When have you been hurt or hurt someone else because limits were not put on behavior?

4. What behavior currently affecting you, if any, do you need to put limits on?

VIDEO SEGMENT
More Lessons in the Laws of Boundaries

- Law #3 is the Law of Power. The words of the apostle Paul
  in Romans 7:15–23 reveal the powerlessness of us human
  beings over our addictions, our unhealthy patterns, and our
  sinful ways. Though you do not have the power in and of
  yourself to overcome your sinful patterns, you do have the
  power to do some things that will bring fruits of victory
  later. Law #3 identifies those powers:

  1. You have the power to agree with the truth about your
     problems (confession).
  2. You have the power to submit your inability to God and
     turn your life over to him, the Doctor who can do what
     you are unable to do—bring about change (1 John 1:9;
     James 4:7–10; Matt. 5:3, 6).
  3. You have the power to ask God and others to reveal
     more and more about what is within your boundaries.
  4. You have the power to turn from the evil that you find
     within you (repentance).
  5. You have the power to humble yourself and ask God and
     others to help you with your developmental injuries and
     leftover childhood needs.
  6. You have the power to seek out those whom you have
     injured and make amends.
  7. You have the power to forgive those who have hurt you.

- Law #4 is the Law of Respect. We need to respect the
  boundaries of others in order to earn respect for our own.
  We need to treat their boundaries the way we want them to
  treat ours. It's the Golden Rule of Matthew 7:12 where
  Jesus said, "So in everything, do to others what you would
  have them do to you." We need to respect the boundaries of

others. When we accept other people's freedom (including their freedom to say no), we don't get angry, feel guilty, or withdraw our love when they set boundaries with us. When we walk in the Spirit and accept others' freedom, we are also free (2 Cor. 3:17).

- Law #5, the Law of Motivation, says: "freedom first, service second." In Matthew 20:26, Jesus calls us to serve, and he modeled a life of service when he walked this earth. But many people serve because they fear that they will lose love or that people will be angry with them if they don't serve. If people serve out of these or any other false motive, they are doomed to failure. If people serve freely out of gratitude, an overflowing heart, and love for others, they realize that it truly is more blessed to give than to receive (Acts 20:35). The Law of Motivation calls us to give bountifully and freely out of a heart of gratitude, rather than a heart of fear.

LET'S TALK
More Lessons in the Laws of Boundaries

Directions

1. Turn to the person next to you and take 10 minutes to talk through the questions listed under the Law of Power, the Law of Respect, and the Law of Motivation. As you do, be thinking about an action step you'll want to take toward the healthy boundaries to which the laws point.

2. After the 10 minutes are up, take 6 minutes on your own to go through and think about the "Boundary Building" questions on page 45 of your Participant's Guide. These questions should challenge you, on a more personal level, to put into practice what you are learning about boundaries.

Law #3: The Law of Power

1. Read through what Paul says in Romans 7:15–23. What phrases can you especially identify with? When have you felt this kind of powerlessness? Be specific about the sin, unhealthy habit, or addiction.

2. What powers listed on page 40 surprise you? encourage you? intimidate you?

3. Explain why these powers to do certain specific things will bring fruits of victory later.

Law #4: The Law of Respect

1. In Matthew 7:12 Jesus said, "So in everything, do to others what you would have them do to you." In light of this command, what can you do to show respect for someone's boundaries?

2. Explain why our acceptance of other people's freedom to set their own boundaries is freeing for us.

3. Why would someone's respect for your boundaries be empowering?

Law #5: The Law of Motivation

1. Jesus calls us to serve (Matt. 20:26). But many people serve out of guilt or because they fear that they will lose love or that people will be angry with them if they don't serve. Other false motives for serving are attempting to avoid loneliness; thinking that to love means always to say yes; thinking that "good" people always say yes; trying to overcome the guilt inside and feel good about themselves; paying back all that they have received; trying to gain people's approval (especially people who represent their parents whose approval was withheld); and overidentifying with the other's loss and feeling the sadness they think their no would cause. What life experiences and early relationships can help engender false motives of service? Give two or three examples.

2. When have you experienced that it truly is more blessed to give than to receive (Acts 20:35)? Be specific about the circumstances and your feelings.

BOUNDARY BUILDING ————————

Law #3: The Law of Power

1. What powers listed on page 40 of this Participant's Guide do you need to begin exercising in your life?

2. What is the first step you will take—today—to exercise one of the powers you just listed? Whom will you ask to help you?

Law #4: The Law of Respect

1. With whom have you been caught up in a fear cycle and therefore been afraid to set the boundaries you need to set? With whom do you comply rather than set boundaries?

2. Whose boundaries do you need to have more respect for? To whom do you need to, in the spirit of Jesus, grant the freedom to be himself or herself and different from you (2 Cor. 3:17)?

Law #5: The Law of Motivation

1. Which, if any, of your "doing" and sacrificing are motivated not by love, but by fear that you won't be loved or fear of anger if you don't comply?

2. What step will you take toward letting God work on your fear or guilt or other false motivations for serving?

SUGGESTED READING ─────────

For more thoughts on this session's topic, read the first half of chapter 5 in *Boundaries*: "Ten Laws of Boundaries." For a more thorough self-evaluation, look at the first part of chapter 3 in the *Boundaries Workbook*.

The Laws of Boundaries, Part II

OVERVIEW

In this session you will

- Discover more about what the Bible says about how boundaries should operate in our lives

- Learn further how boundaries can be developed all through our lives

VIDEO SEGMENT
Laws #6 and #7

- Things can hurt but not harm us. In fact, things that hurt can even be good for us. And things that feel good can be very harmful to us.

- Law #6 is the Law of Evaluation: We need to evaluate the effects of setting boundaries and be responsible to the other person, but that does not mean we should avoid setting boundaries because someone might respond with hurt or anger.

- Just as iron sharpens iron (Prov. 27:17), we need confrontation and truth from others to grow. No one likes to hear negative things about him- or herself, but in the long run, hearing those things may be good for us (Eph. 4:25; Prov. 27:6).

- We need to evaluate the painful effects caused by setting boundaries and by the confrontations that come with enforcing those boundaries, and we need to see how that hurt is helpful.

- Law #7 is the Law of Proactivity. Just as in the physical world, in the spiritual realm of human relationships, for every action, there is an equal and opposite reaction (Rom. 4:15; 5:20; 7:5; Eph. 6:4; Col. 3:21). After years of compliance, for instance, a person's pent-up rage may explode. Reactive phases like that are necessary for the establishment of boundaries, but not sufficient.

- Proactive people show what they love, what they want, what they purpose, and what they stand for—as opposed to those who are known by what they hate, what they don't like, what they stand against, and what they will not do. Proactive people are able to "love others as themselves," "die to self," and not "return evil for evil."

LET'S TALK
Laws #6 and #7

Directions

1. Divide into six groups.

2. Each group will be assigned one question about Law #6 or Law #7 for discussion. When we come back together, a spokesperson from each group will share that group's ideas with the rest of us.

3. You will have 5 minutes to complete this exercise.

Law #6: The Law of Evaluation

1. Explain the difference between hurting and harming someone.

2. What kinds of healthy boundaries may cause pain to other people? Give two or three specific examples.

3. When has someone protected his or her boundaries and done something that hurt you? Did that action harm you?

BOUNDARY BUILDING ————

What current circumstances call for you to set boundaries? If you set boundaries, what pain or disappointment might you cause someone you love? Will that pain harm the person?

Law #7: The Law of Proactivity

1. What are the benefits of reactive phases, those stages when people react against oppression, victimization, emotional blackmail, manipulation, and other abusive situations?

2. Why must such reactive phases necessarily be limited? Consider what Paul says in Galatians 5:13, 15.

3. Proactive people show what they love, what they want, what they purpose, and what they stand for—as opposed to those who are known by what they hate, what they don't like, what they stand against, and what they will not do. What benefits come with being proactive? Give a few real-life examples.

BOUNDARY BUILDING ────

Where are you on the continuum between proactive and reactive as described in the preceding question? In what relationship(s) is it time for you to move past the reactive to the proactive and begin living out the power of love? Make this a matter for prayer.

VIDEO SEGMENT
Laws #8, #9, and #10

- Law #8 is the Law of Envy. Boundaryless people feel empty and unfulfilled. They look at another's sense of fullness and feel envious (Gal. 6:4). That time and energy need to be spent on taking responsibility for their lack and doing something about it.

- Envy should always be a sign to us that we are lacking something. At that moment, we need to ask God to help us understand what we resent, why we do not have whatever we are envying, and whether we truly need it. We should ask him to show us how to get there or to help us grieve what we cannot have and be content with what we do have.

- Law #9 is the Law of Activity. Many times we have boundary problems because we lack initiative—the God-given ability to propel ourselves into life. God wants us to be assertive and active, seeking and knocking on the door of life. The sin that God rebukes is not trying and failing, but failing to try (Luke 19:12–27). "Just do it!" should be more than a tennis shoe advertisement! Trying, failing, and trying again is called learning.

- Evil is an active force, and passivity can become an ally of evil by not pushing against it. We are to actively work to preserve our souls. That is the role of boundaries: they define and preserve our property, our soul. And our boundaries can be created only by our being active and aggressive, by our knocking, seeking, and asking. So we need to move out of passivity by taking initiative to set healthy boundaries.

- Law #10 is the Law of Exposure. As we've said in this series, a boundary defines where an individual begins and ends. The Law of Exposure says that our boundaries need to be made visible to others and communicated to them in relationships (Eph. 4:25–26; 5:13–14).

- We have many boundary problems because of relational fears—fears of guilt, of not being liked, of the loss of love, loss of connection, loss of approval, of receiving anger, of being known, and so on. These relational problems can be solved only in relationships, for that is the context of the problems themselves.

- The Law of Exposure acknowledges that our boundaries are affected by sin and that they need to be brought into the light for God to heal them and for others to benefit from them. This is the path to real love: communicating your boundaries openly.

LET'S TALK
Laws #8, #9, and #10

Directions

1. You will have 10 minutes to answer a few questions about yourself in light of Laws #8, #9, and #10.

2. At the end of the 10 minutes, turn to someone near you and take 5 minutes to talk together about what you will do to establish and enforce boundaries that grow out of these three laws.

Law #8: The Law of Envy

1. What things and what people do you tend to envy most? What does your answer show you about yourself?

2. What step will you take toward getting what you lack? What might God be calling you to do about that lack?

Law #9: The Law of Activity

1. How easy or difficult it is for you to take initiative in life? When have you seen, in someone's life or perhaps your own,

passivity become an ally of evil by not pushing against it? In what aspect of your life are you failing to try right now?

2. Where is God calling you, through this discussion, to be more active? Where will you begin to knock, seek, and ask? Be specific. What baby step will you take to begin exercising your "initiative muscle"?

Law #10: The Law of Exposure

1. With whom do you struggle to communicate your boundaries? Why? What aspects of yourself do you hide? Why?

2. With which safe person in your life will you begin to share the hidden parts of yourself? With whom will you start trying to communicate your boundaries? If appropriate, ask God to bring into your life someone safe with whom you can gradually begin to share all of yourself and communicate openly.

VIDEO SEGMENT
What We've Learned

Each of us *can* learn from God's Word the principles for healthy boundaries. We can also rely on his guidance and his Spirit to help us fight the battles that will occur as we strive to make God's ways part of our character. God has brought us out from an alien land, and he is teaching us his ways.

SUGGESTED READING ────────

For more thoughts on this session's topic, read the second half of chapter 5 in *Boundaries*: "Ten Laws of Boundaries." For a more thorough self-evaluation, look at the second half of chapter 3 in the *Boundaries Workbook*.

Myths About Boundaries

OVERVIEW

In this session you will

- Look at eight myths about boundaries

- Investigate which myths about boundaries you have accepted as truth

- Learn what you can do to get free of those myths that entangle and ensnare you

VIDEO SEGMENT
Myths About Boundaries

- *Myth #1: If I set boundaries, I'm being selfish.* Boundaries don't turn us from other-centeredness to self-centeredness. Instead, boundaries actually increase our ability to care about others.

- *Myth #2: Boundaries are a sign of disobedience.* In reality, a *lack* of boundaries is often a sign of disobedience. We must establish boundaries because, among other reasons, if we can't say no, we can't say yes.

- *Myth #3: If I begin setting boundaries, I will be hurt by others.* Boundaries are a "litmus test" for the quality of our relationships. Those people in our lives who can respect our boundaries will love our wills, our opinions, our separateness.

- *Myth #4: If I set boundaries, I will hurt others.* Boundaries are not an offensive weapon, but a defensive tool. They simply prevent our treasures from being taken at the wrong time.

- *Myth #5: Boundaries mean I am angry.* Boundaries themselves don't cause anger in us. But anger is a sign that our boundaries have been violated, that we don't have boundaries, or that we need to confront the threat. Anger also provides us with a sense of power to solve a problem.

- *Myth #6: When others set boundaries, it injures me.* If we want others to respect our boundaries, then we must be willing to respect the boundaries of others.

- *Myth #7: Boundaries cause feelings of guilt.* God doesn't allow the issues of gratitude and boundaries to be confused, and neither should we. Our feelings of gratitude need not obligate us to fail to set boundaries with those who have given gifts to us.

- *Myth #8: Boundaries are permanent, and I'm afraid of burning my bridges.* It's important to understand that your no is always subject to you. You own your boundaries; they don't own you. You can renegotiate or change a boundary when you are in a safer place.

LET'S TALK
Debunking the Myths

Directions

1. We'll begin by counting off from one to eight to form eight groups: the people who were ones will discuss the first myth; the twos, the second myth; and so on.

2. Discuss the questions asked about the myth to which your group was assigned (see pages 63–70). Be sure to appoint a spokesperson to share your ideas with the rest of the group in a 2-minute summary of the highlights of your discussion.

3. You will have 10 minutes to complete this exercise.

Myth #1: If I set boundaries, I'm being selfish

1. Explain why setting healthy boundaries is a matter of healthy stewardship of the life God has given us rather than ungodly selfishness.

2. What do verses like Matthew 7:7, Matthew 25:13, Philippians 2:12–13, and 2 Corinthians 5:10 suggest about what we are responsible for?

3. Why do appropriate boundaries actually increase our ability to care about others? Give two or three specific examples.

BOUNDARY BUILDING ───────

In what current relationship would clearer, stronger boundaries enable you to be a stronger, more caring participant?

Myth #2: Boundaries are a sign of disobedience

1. In 2 Corinthians 9:7, we read about the attitude of obedience which pleases God. What does this verse suggest about those times when we say yes but mean no? An internal no nullifies an external yes (Hos. 6:6)!

2. While we find ourselves living under various authorities, our disobedience to them is ultimately disobedience to God. Give an example of when a lack of boundaries can be a sign of such disobedience. Hint: Consider saying no to good things for wrong reasons.

BOUNDARY BUILDING ————————

Reflect on a commitment you made with an external yes despite your internal no. Did you fulfill that commitment? If so, with what attitude? Where are you currently acting out of fear ("reluctantly" and "under compulsion" [2 Cor. 9:7]) rather than love (1 John 4:18)?

Myth #3: If I begin setting boundaries, I will be hurt by others

1. Why are boundaries a "litmus test" for the quality of our relationships? What do we learn when a person has trouble respecting our boundaries and accepting our no, seeming to love us only when we say yes (Luke 6:26)?

2. The Bible clearly distinguishes between those who love truth (the "wise" and "righteous") and those who don't (Prov. 10:23; Phil. 4:8). How is setting limits or establishing boundaries akin to telling the truth? Consider the fact that God is more concerned about our heart than our outward compliance. Why might people close to us be threatened when we establish boundaries? What role can safe places of being "rooted and grounded in love" (Eph. 3:17 NASB) play as a person learns to tell the truth?

BOUNDARY BUILDING ———————

Setting boundaries is a way to tell the truth about who you are. When has setting boundaries led to increased intimacy in a relationship? Consider in what relationship you need to establish some boundaries today. What do you feel the risks are? When will you take a bold step of setting limits? Who will be there to support you with prayer?

Myth #4: If I set boundaries, I will hurt others

1. Explain what is meant by the statement "Boundaries are a defensive tool rather than an offensive weapon." Consider Proverbs 4:23.

2. Some people may fear that they will hurt others by establishing and maintaining boundaries because they project their own wounded or sad parts onto those other people and over-identify with their perhaps nonexistent pain. These people feel that if they have limits, they are not being loving and are in fact being hurtful. When has your concern that your no would hurt someone kept you from establishing or maintaining boundaries? What feelings and experiences do you think lay behind your concern?

3. Why is it important to have a group of supportive relationships? What can happen if you are relying on God and on just one best friend? When we've taken the responsibility to develop several supportive relationships in a biblical fashion (Eph. 4:2–3), why are we better able to handle someone's no?

BOUNDARY BUILDING ————————

There are times when, for some reason or another, people can't sacrifice and help us, even when our needs are legitimate. Even Jesus left the multitudes, for example, to be alone with his Father (Matt. 14:22–23). In light of this perspective, how do you want to respond—internally and externally—the next time someone maintains appropriate boundaries and leaves you to look elsewhere to get your needs met?

Myth #5: Boundaries mean I am angry

1. Explore why beginning to set limits might put you in touch with some feelings of old anger. Then explain how anger—which signals that our boundaries have been violated and which provides us with a sense of power to solve a problem—can be an ally (look at Jesus in John 2:13–17).

2. It takes years to dissipate anger stemming from years of no's that were never voiced, never respected, and never listened to. Why does establishing boundaries decrease and even prevent some anger? Consider the "early warning system" function of anger.

BOUNDARY BUILDING ─────────

Do you let yourself experience anger? Why or why not? If you do, how do you deal with it? When has anger energized you to confront someone or set a limit? Be specific about what you were protecting or the problem you were solving. Finally, are you aware of "old anger" inside your heart? If so, what are you doing to work through it appropriately? How do you want to deal with anger without sinning against someone (Eph. 4:26, 31)?

Myth #6: When others set boundaries, it injures me

1. Why would having inappropriate boundaries set on us, especially in childhood, injure us and make it hard to accept people's boundaries?

2. We may be unable to receive someone's boundary if we have made that person too important. What might this unhealthy situation look like in a marriage?

3. An inability to accept others' boundaries can indicate a problem in taking responsibility. Why would being rescued lead to this kind of irresponsibility?

4. If you feel hurt by someone's boundaries—by someone saying no—what kind of old hurt could be behind your present pain? What could a person do to resolve that kind of pain?

5. Read what Jesus says in Matthew 7:12. What does this rule say to you about boundaries?

BOUNDARY BUILDING ──────────

When Paul set limits on the Corinthians' rebelliousness, they responded with sorrow and repentance (2 Cor. 7:8–9). Describe a situation in your world where setting boundaries—either you setting boundaries for yourself or someone maintaining their boundaries in their relationship with you—could lead to repentance.

Myth #7: Boundaries cause feelings of guilt

1. One of the major obstacles to setting boundaries with others in our lives is our feelings of obligation: the idea that because we have received something, we owe something. God's gift of salvation cost us his Son (John 3:16). What does Colossians 2:7 suggest about how we should respond to that ultimate gift—and any other gift as well? What is going on with the giver when intangible gifts (love, time, energy) are given with strings attached?

2. As the Revelation letters to the churches of Ephesus, Pergamum, and Thyatira illustrate, God doesn't allow validation and boundaries to be confused. Although he validates the churches and praises their accomplishments for the kingdom, he does indeed set boundaries with them by confronting their irresponsibilities (Rev. 2:4, 14, 20). Why aren't validation and boundaries mutually exclusive? Why are they so easily confused and interwoven?

BOUNDARY BUILDING ————————

Where have feelings of obligation prevented you from setting boundaries? What have been the consequences of your failure to set boundaries in that situation? Are you, for instance, stuck at home, in school, church, a job, or a friendship? What relationship is God calling you to set boundaries in, despite what that person has given you?

Myth #8: Boundaries are permanent, and I'm afraid of burning my bridges

1. The Bible shows us many instances when boundaries were renegotiated and changed (Jonah 3:10 and Acts 15:37–39, together with 2 Tim. 4:11). Boundaries—which you can always change—can help preserve a relationship, and temporary boundaries can bring people back together. Give at least one example of each of these situations.

2. Why is it important to recognize the difference between owning our boundaries and being owned by them? Which option gives power and freedom to grow?

BOUNDARY BUILDING ————

What boundaries have you failed to set out of fear that they would be permanent? What boundaries are you more willing to set now that you know they needn't be permanent?

ON YOUR OWN
Reflections

Directions

Take 5 minutes to reflect on what you have learned today and to answer the questions you see below.

1. What is the most helpful thing you heard today?

2. At this point, what is your greatest fear about setting boundaries? How, if at all, have the truths discussed today eased that fear?

3. Where in your life right now do you most need boundaries? What have you determined to do as a result of what you've learned today about God's truth, boundaries, and yourself?

SUGGESTED READING ───────────

For more thoughts on this session's topic, read chapter 6 in *Boundaries*: "Common Boundary Myths." For a more thorough self-evaluation, look at chapter 4 in the *Boundaries Workbook*.

Boundary Conflicts, Part I

OVERVIEW

In this session you will

- Look at some potential boundary conflicts within yourself and with God

- Determine what healthy action you can take to avoid or deal with these potential boundary conflicts

VIDEO SEGMENT
Boundary Conflicts, Part I

- In this session we'll look at seven common areas of internal boundary conflicts:

    1. *Eating:* Do you use food as a false boundary, to avoid intimacy by gaining weight and becoming less attractive? Do you binge, finding the comfort of food less scary than the prospect of real relationships (1 John 4:18)?

    2. *Money:* Do you struggle with impulse spending, careless budgeting, living beyond your means, credit problems, chronic borrowing from friends, ineffectual savings plans, or working more to pay all the bills? How could your love of money be the root of evil in your life (1 Tim. 6:10)?

    3. *Time management:* How do you deal with deadlines? Are you a do-ahead person or a last-minute person? How well do you manage your time (Eph. 5:16)?

    4. *Task completion:* Are you a good starter but a poor finisher (Prov. 21:5)? Have you started an exercise program, a diet, a Bible study program, or a Scripture memorization plan several times and never gotten very far?

    5. *The tongue:* Are you pleased with how often you use your tongue to bless others? Or do you use your tongue too frequently for nonstop talking, dominating conversations, gossiping, being sarcastic, threatening, flattering, or seducing (Prov. 10:19; 17:27; Matt. 12:36)?

    6. *Sexuality:* Are you caught up in any out-of-control sexual behavior (Eph. 5:8–11)?

    7. *Alcohol/substance abuse:* Are you abusing drugs and/or alcohol (1 Cor. 3:16–17)? Are you being honest with your-

self as you evaluate your use? Are you dealing with divorce, job loss, financial havoc, or medical problems because of your use of alcohol and/or drugs?

- There are at least three reasons why our no's don't work in these seven areas.

  1. We are responsible *for*—not just *to*—the person with the problem when we are that person. We *are* responsible for ourselves. Simply saying no to ourselves in an attempt to establish boundaries isn't enough because of the unmet needs, unrecognized fear, or unresolved pain driving the unhealthy behavior we want to eliminate. We need to truly own the problem and its roots and take responsibility for ourselves, for dealing with our unmet needs, unrecognized fear, and unresolved pain.

  2. Due to shame, fear, or our own self-sufficiency, we tend to withdraw from relationships and accountability when it comes to dealing with situations like these. Self-boundary problems worsen with increased aloneness (James 5:16).

  3. We try to use willpower to solve our boundary problems. If all we need is our will to overcome the evil within us, we certainly don't need a Savior (1 Cor. 1:17).

- We have personal boundaries in our relationship with God. He respects those boundaries—and we need to respect his.

- God respects our boundaries by leaving work for us to do that only we can do (Matt. 25:13–29; Phil. 2:12); by allowing us to experience the painful consequences of our behavior so that we will change and not perish (Ezek. 18:23; 2 Peter 3:9); and by respecting our no when that is our response to him (Matt. 19:16–22; Luke 15:11–24).

- God respects our boundaries, and he expects us to respect his. If we are to have a real relationship with him, we need to respect his right and freedom to say no to us. But God does not want us to be passive in our relationship with him, either. In fact, he asks us to be tenacious in trying to persuade him to change his mind. Sometimes, through dialogue with us, he does change his mind (Gen. 18:16–33; Luke 11:5–9; 18:1–8).

- However God responds to our requests, we are to respect his wishes and stay in relationship with him.

BOUNDARY CONFLICTS
WITH GOD

- When we consider boundaries and God, we need to keep in mind that_____is what the gospel is all about. The news of Jesus Christ dying on the cross for your sins and mine is a gospel of_____ _____; it brings hostile parties together and heals relationships between God and humanity and between people.

- Boundaries are inherent in any relationship (even our relationship with God), for boundaries define the two parties who are loving each other. Boundaries help us see God as he really is. They enable us to negotiate life, fulfilling our responsibilities. If we are trying to do God's work for him, we will_____. If we are wishing for him to do our work for us, he will_____. But if we do our work and God does his, we will find _____in a real relationship with our Creator.

LET'S TALK
Steps Toward Healthy Self-Boundaries

Directions

1. Divide into groups of four or five.

2. On pages 79–80 you will find several steps for resolving boundary conflicts.

3. Working with one of the hypothetical situations given below, walk through the subsequent questions toward resolution of that conflict.

4. Be sure to choose a spokesperson to share one or two highlights of your group's discussion with the large group.

5. You'll have 20 minutes to complete this exercise.

Hypothetical situations

1. Workaholism

2. An inability to maintain a relationship with a member of the opposite sex (this person always does the loving; the other person, the leaving)

3. Anger that emerges at inappropriate times and in inappropriate ways

Steps Toward Resolving Boundary Conflicts

1. *Identify the symptoms.* What destructive fruit (depression, anxiety, panic, phobias, rage, relationship struggles, isolation, work problems, psychosomatic problems) are you experiencing because you are not able to say no to yourself?

2. *Identify the root causes of the symptoms.*
Possible causes:

- Lack of training in setting limits, facing consequences for your actions, or delaying gratification
- Rewarded destructiveness: learning that out-of-control behavior brings relationships
- A distortion of legitimate, God-given needs
- Fear of relationships—and your out-of-control behavior keeps people away
- A deep hunger for love that was unmet in the first few years of your life
- Being raised in a legalistic environment—and you are now rebelling
- Covering emotional hurt that came when you were neglected or abused as a child
- Emotional hurt in adult life

3. *Identify the boundary conflict.*

- Do you have weak or nonexistent boundaries in relation to eating, money, time, task completion, the tongue, sexuality, or alcohol and substance abuse? Ask God for insight into what other areas of your life are out of control.
- Why won't sheer willpower alone work in resolving this conflict?

4. *Identify who needs to take responsibility.* Your behavior pattern may be directly traceable to family problems, neglect, abuse, or trauma. Even so, explain what it means that you are responsible for your boundary conflicts.

5. *Identify what you need as you proceed along this path.* You are severely hampered in gaining either insight into or control over yourself when you are disconnected from God's people. Safe, trusting, grace-and-truth relationships are spiritual and emotional fuel. What relationships are giving you this fuel? Where can you go to begin establishing such relationships?

6. *"Just Do It."* How do you begin? What step do you need to take—and when will you take it? If, for instance, you missed out on your father's approval or your mother's love, what good people can offer you affirmation and love now? Find such people.

   Other possible steps:
   - Setting limits with safe people (begin learning assertiveness, confrontation, and honesty in a support group)
   - Saying no to the bad (what habits or compulsions do you need to renounce, repent of, and not do anymore?) and forgiving the people in your life you need to forgive
   - Address your real need (often out-of-control patterns disguise a need for something else); allow yourself to fail (embrace and learn from failure)
   - Listen to empathic feedback from others (let other believers provide perspective and support)
   - Welcome consequences as a teacher
   - Surround yourself with people who are loving and supportive

7. *What accountability and consequences do you need to build into your program?* You might want to contract with a friend to make sure consequences happen: you agree, for instance, that if you fall back into the unhealthy behavior, you'll pay him or her ten dollars.

A FEW FINAL NOTES

- Learning to be mature in self-boundaries is not easy. Many obstacles hinder our progress; however, God desires our

  _____ and _____ even more than we do.

  He's on our team as an exhorter, _____, and implorer;

  as _____, Redeemer, and loving Father.

- Allow yourself to _____. Listen to the empathic _____

  of friends. Welcome _____ of your new behav-

  iors. Surround yourself with people who are _____

  and _____.

- One last reminder. The formula we've looked at for developing

  self-boundaries is _____. That is, as you deal with

  _____ _____, _____, get empathic

  _____, suffer _____, and

  are _____, you build stronger internal boundaries

  each time. As you stay with your goal and with the right people,

  you will build a sense of _____ that can truly

  become part of your _____ for life.

SUGGESTED READING ——————

For more thoughts on this session's topic, read chapters 12 and 13 in *Boundaries*: "Boundaries and Your Self" and "Boundaries and God." For a more thorough self-evaluation, look at chapters 10 and 11 in the *Boundaries Workbook*.

Boundary Conflicts, Part II

OVERVIEW

In this session you will

- Use principles already learned to establish boundaries with family, friends, spouse, children, and coworkers

- Discover that these five boundary conflicts are, at heart, issues of self-control rather than "other-control"

VIDEO SEGMENT
Boundary Conflicts, Part II

- Today we'll look at how to establish boundaries with family, friends, spouse, children, and coworkers. Each of these five areas of boundary conflicts is, at heart, an issue of self-control rather than other-control.

Boundaries and Your Family

Susie made choices *on the outside*, but *on the inside*, things were different. Susie, and others like her, do not really "own" themselves. People who own their lives do not feel guilty when they make choices. They take other people into consideration, but when they make choices for the wishes of others, they are choosing out of love, not guilt; to advance a good, not to avoid being bad.

Boundaries and Your Friends

Sean and Tim: The result of two compliants interacting is that neither does what he really wants. Each is so afraid of telling the other the truth that neither ever does.

Bill and Scott: The aggressive controller has no problem demanding or sometimes simply taking what he wants. "I need it" is enough reason for the aggressive controller to help himself to whatever the compliant has, be it car keys, a cup of sugar, or three hours of time.

Cathy and Sharon: Sharon is not consciously trying to manipulate her compliant friend. However, no matter what her good intentions are, when she's in a jam, Sharon uses her friends. She takes them for granted, thinking they shouldn't mind doing her a favor. Her friends go along, saying, "Well, that's just Sharon." They stifle their resentment.

Marsha and Tammy: One friend doing all the work and the other coasting illustrates the compliant/nonresponsive conflict. One party feels frustrated and resentful; the other wonders what the problem is. Marsha senses that the friendship isn't as important to Tammy as it is to her.

Boundaries and Your Spouse

Margo and Rob: One of the most important elements that promotes intimacy between two people is the ability of each to take responsibility for his or her own *feelings*.

Jim and Michelle: Both Jim and Michelle had needs. Problems arise when we make someone else responsible for our needs and *desires* and when we blame them for our disappointments.

Bob and Nancy: Our spouse is not responsible for our *limits*; we are. Only we know what we can and want to give, and only we can be responsible for drawing that line. If we do not draw it, we can quickly become resentful.

Boundaries and Your Children

How we approach boundaries and childrearing will have an enormous impact on the character of our kids. If we teach responsibility, limit setting, and delay of gratification early on, the smoother our children's later years of life will be.

Boundaries and Work

Favors and sacrifices are part of the Christian life; enabling is not. Learn to tell the difference by seeing if your giving is helping the other to become better or worse. The Bible requires responsible action out of the one who is given to. If you do not see it after a season, set limits!

- Boundary conflicts you encounter can be solved by taking specific steps.

  1. *Identify the symptom.*

  2. *Identify the origins or root causes of the symptom* (unmet needs, unrecognized fears, and unresolved fears, etc.).

  3. *Identify the boundary conflict.* Consider, for instance, what "law of boundaries" is being violated, who is taking responsibility for whom, or what consequences aren't being enforced.

  4. *Identify who needs to take responsibility* in the situation and *the need that drives the conflict.*

  5. *Take in the good.* God is willing to meet your needs through his people, but you must humble yourself, reach out to a good support system, and take in the good offered to you. Learn to respond to and receive love even if you're clumsy at first.

  6. *Practice setting limits with safe people.* Begin saying no by practicing with people in your support group who will love and respect your boundaries.

  7. *Say no to the bad.* Avoid hurtful situations and people who abused and controlled you in the past.

  8. *Forgive.* Setting people who have hurt you free from an old debt is to stop wanting something from them; it sets you free as well.

LET'S TALK
Boundary Building

Directions

1. On your own, choose one of the five categories of boundaries covered in this session.

2. Take 15 minutes to read through the questions for the category you chose. Answer as many as you have time for, then write down one thing you have learned about yourself and one goal you have set for yourself.

3. After 15 minutes, turn to someone near you and take 5 minutes to share with each other what you learned about yourself or the goal you have set for yourself.

Boundaries and Your Family

1. What choices have you made that your parents let you know, in one way or another, they don't fully approve of? Have you made these choices on the inside as well as the outside? Or do you feel guilty, apologetic, or uneasy about your choices?

2. Where do you need to loosen ties with your family of origin? What specific steps will you take to strengthen ties or forge new ones with the family that was created by your marriage?

3. Are you an adult financially? Support your answer with specific details about your life. What, if any, life management functions are you allowing your parents to still perform for you?

4. *Triangulation* is a term which refers to the failure to resolve a conflict between two persons and the pulling in of a third to take sides. Is this a pattern in your family of origin that you've carried into your adult life? What conflict do you need to resolve directly right now?

5. Do you feel responsible for your parents? Is it unhealthy or is it a biblical, healthy responsibility (1 Tim. 5:3–4)? Are you still holding an allegiance to your earthly parents or have you fully become part of God's family and are now obeying his ways (Matt. 12:46–50; 23:9; Gal. 4:1–7)? Give specific evidence supporting your answer.

6. What is God saying to you personally through this lesson about boundaries, families of origin, and the family you've entered by marriage? And what will you do in response?

    Lesson I learned about myself: _____

    _____

    Boundary-building goal: _____

    _____

Boundaries and Your Friends

1. What role do you tend to take in a friendship—compliant, avoidant, manipulative, or nonresponsive?

2. What does Romans 8:1 suggest about a strong basis for a friendship? When has being "in Christ Jesus" strengthened one of your friendships? When, for instance, has it helped you weather the storm of disappointment, hurt, or even betrayal? Be specific.

3. What keeps you connected to your friends? their performance? their lovability? your guilt? your sense of obligation? something else? See 1 John 4:12.

4. In what relationship(s) have you been the minister, the rescuer, the strong one without needs? Why do you think you chose that role for yourself? In what relationship(s) have you been able to ask for things for yourself (James 4:2)? What did you ask for and receive? If you don't yet feel comfortable asking for things you need, find a safe relationship where you can learn and practice this skill.

5. In what friendship have you become aware of or been confronted about your self-centeredness? Describe that interaction and how you have benefited from that uncomfortable but important lesson about yourself.

6. What is God saying to you personally through this lesson about boundaries, ministries, and nurturing friendships? And what will you do in response?

    Lesson I learned about myself: _____

    _____

    Boundary-building goal: _____

    _____

Boundaries and Your Spouse

1. What feelings are you able to express in your marriage (2 Cor. 6:13)? What feelings would you like to be able to express? What do you tend to do rather than express your feelings to your spouse? How does that behavior affect your relationship with your spouse? What feelings do you need to take responsibility for today and share with your spouse?

2. Like feelings, desires are another element of personhood for which each spouse needs to take responsibility (James 4:1–2). What conflicting wants do you and your spouse need to work out?

3. Often spouses will do more than they really want to and then resent the other for not stopping them from overgiving. Where do you need to set some limits in what you will give your spouse? Where do you need to take responsibility for your own wants instead of expecting your spouse to take care of them all for you?

4. Which of your actions, if any, is your spouse not letting you suffer the consequences for? What actions do you need to let your spouse suffer the consequences for? What is keeping you from letting your spouse suffer the consequences for his or her behavior?

5. Where are you waiting to be rescued rather than taking responsibility for yourself? Where are you giving in to your spouse's anger, pouting, and disappointments and thereby taking responsibility for what he/she is feeling? Where are you rescuing your spouse (see Prov. 19:19)? Explain the difference between being responsible *to* your spouse and responsible *for* him or her. Where do you need to show responsibility in your marriage today? What evil do you see and need to confront?

6. Where are you not respecting your spouse's boundaries, feelings, or choices? In what ways are you being controlling?

7. What is God saying to you personally through this lesson about boundaries, communication, and your spouse? And what will you do in response?

   Lesson I learned about myself: _____

   _____

   Boundary-building goal: _____

   _____

Boundaries and Your Children

1. How old are your children? What have they learned about
   boundaries up to this point? How do your children respond
   when others set limits on them? Do they have a tantrum or
   sulk? Do they comply in order to keep the peace?

2. What are you doing to teach your children responsibility,
   limit setting, and delay of gratification?

3. The positive facets of discipline are proactivity, prevention,
   and instruction (Eph. 6:4). Give specific examples of discipline that uses each of these positive aspects and make
   them appropriate to the age and behaviors of your children.
   The negative facets of discipline are correction, chastise-
   ment, and consequences (Prov. 15:10). Now give specific
   examples of discipline using each of these negative aspects
   and again make them appropriate to the age and behaviors
   of your children. Now give an example of how you could use
   consequences to help set limits for your children. Use a specific situation you are currently dealing with.

4. What is your understanding of the difference between discipline (Heb. 12:10) and punishment (Rom. 6:23; James 2:10)? In what areas are your children currently practicing setting boundaries? How is your discipline helping them? Where could you be using consequences to give your children the chance to practice and learn?

5. What does it mean to you and your efforts that God will not judge you or withdraw his love from you? As they practice the various skills of life, do your children know that you will not judge them or withdraw your love from them? Support your answer.

6. What is God saying to you personally through this lesson about boundaries, your parenting, and your children? What will you do in response?

    Lesson I learned about myself: _____

    _____

    Boundary-building goal: _____

    _____

Boundaries and Work

1. What work do you do? What does Paul command believers
    in Colossians 3:23? How could doing your work as "for the
    Lord" impact, if not revolutionize, your work?

2. What aspects of your work reflect the activities God does?
    How is God using your work to make you more Christlike?

3. What problems in the workplace are you currently facing?

    - Getting saddled with another person's responsibilities
    - Working too much overtime
    - Misplaced priorities when you're on the job
    - Difficult coworkers
    - Critical attitudes
    - Conflict with authority
    - Expecting too much of work
    - Taking work-related stress home
    - Disliking your job

4. Consider what you are learning about boundaries in this
    study. What lessons can you apply to the situation(s) you
    identified?

5. God wants you to discover and use your gifts to his glory. He will also hold you accountable for what you do. What promise do you find in Psalm 37:4–5? What warning do you find in Ecclesiastes 11:9?

6. Where are you not respecting the boundaries of your coworkers? In what ways is your laziness, irresponsibility, or disobedience impacting others?

7. What is God saying to you personally through this lesson about boundaries, ministry, and work? And what will you do in response?

    Lesson I learned about myself: _____

    _____

    Boundary-building goal: _____

    _____

THE IMPORTANCE OF ESTABLISHING BOUNDARIES

A Review

- We've seen that we need to make choices on the
  _____ as well as the_____, especially when
  we're trying to separate from our_____ of origin.

- We've looked at what happens in_____when
  people don't have or don't enforce healthy boundaries.

- We saw some_____in trouble because the individuals didn't take responsibility for their_____,
  _____, or_____.

- Gerald and Shannon's experience with Robby reminded us
  that boundaries are important for our_____, too. How
  we approach boundaries and childrearing will have an
  enormous impact on their_____. We need to be
  teaching them_____, _____,
  and_____ _____ _____.

- We also saw that boundaries are critical in the
  _____. We need to do our job at the
  office, and helping others out is part of the Christian life,
  but_____ is not. We must learn to see if
  our_____is helping a coworker to become
  better or worse.

SUGGESTED READING ——————

For more thoughts on this session's topic, read chapters 7–11 in *Boundaries*: "Boundaries and Your Family," "Boundaries and Your Friends," "Boundaries and Your Spouse," "Boundaries and Your Children, and "Boundaries and Work." For a more thorough self-evaluation, look at chapters 5–9 in the *Boundaries Workbook*.

Boundary Successes, Part I

REVIEW OF SESSIONS 1–7

- What new understanding about boundaries, about relationships, or about family dynamics have you gained?

- What "aha!" experience have you had? When did a lightbulb go on?

- What has God shown you about yourself? About himself?

- What practical aspect of the teaching is already making a difference in your life?

- What has been revolutionary or life-changing about our study of boundaries so far?

OVERVIEW

In this session you will

- Learn more about successfully establishing and maintaining healthy boundaries

- Look at six measurements you can take to determine your growth and development toward mature boundaries

VIDEO SEGMENT
Measuring Boundary Growth

Specific, orderly changes herald the emergence of mature boundaries. In fact, you can measure the progression from Point A (boundarylessness) to Point B (mature boundaries). Right now we'll look at six steps you can use to measure your growth in boundary development:

- *Measurement #1: Resentment, our early-warning signal.* One of the first signs that someone is beginning to develop boundaries is a sense of resentment, frustration, or anger at the subtle and not-so-subtle violations in your life. Just as radar signals the approach of a foreign missile, your anger can alert you to boundary violations in your life.

- *Measurement #2: A change of tastes: becoming drawn to boundary-lovers.* As boundary-injured individuals begin developing their own boundaries, they become attracted to people who can hear their no without being critical and without getting hurt—people who will simply say, "Okay. See you next time."

  When we find relationships in which we have freedom to set limits, something wonderful happens. In addition to the freedom to say no, we find the freedom to say a wholehearted, unconflicted, gratitude-driven yes to others.

- *Measurement #3: Joining the family.* Joining the boundaried family is important mainly because, as with any spiritual discipline, boundaries can't be worked on in a vacuum. Furthermore, knowing we have a spiritual and emotional home somewhere helps us keep firm boundaries.

- *Measurement #4: Treasuring our treasures.* In order to further develop and strengthen healthy boundaries, we need to begin to value what we are responsible for—our feelings, talents, thoughts, attitudes, behavior, body, and the resources God has entrusted to us. This valuing—saying that these treasures matter and deciding to pay attention to them—helps us take the steps we need to take to protect those treasures and grow in them. After all, what you value in life is what you will invest in (Matt. 6:21).

- *Measurement #5: Practicing baby no's.* It is important to take baby steps toward communicating our new boundaries. A good place to start is with a support group or good friends. A good, supportive relationship cherishes the no of all parties involved. So start practicing your no with people who will honor it and love you for it.

- *Measurement #6: Rejoicing in the guilty feelings.* A sign that someone is becoming a boundaried person is often a sense of self-condemnation or critical self judgment. The culprit here is an overactive, inaccurate, and unbiblically harsh internal judge. Because of this overactive judge, the boundary-injured individual has great difficulty setting limits. Activating this hostile conscience is a sign of spiritual growth because it means the person is defying an incorrect authority (that hostile conscience) in order to obey God.

LET'S TALK
Measuring Boundary Growth

Directions

1. Divide into six groups.

2. Each group will be assigned one of the Measurements of Growth listed below.

3. In your small group, discuss the one or two questions you find listed under that measurement. If you have time, discuss the "Boundary Building" questions that accompany that measurement as well.

4. When the groups are called back together, a spokesperson from each group will share insights from that group with the large group.

5. You will have 10 minutes to complete this exercise.

Measurement #1: Resentment, our early-warning signal

1. Why is resentment, frustration, or anger a signal that someone has violated one of your boundaries? See Proverbs 29:11.

2. How can anger—unrecognized and unexpressed—affect our day-to-day lives?

BOUNDARY BUILDING ————————

What experiences or relationships have helped or are helping you get in touch with your anger, resentment, or frustration and enabled you to see that you want to be treated differently?

Measurement #2: A change of tastes: becoming drawn to boundary-lovers

1. Define "boundary-buster." Discuss how someone who has difficulty setting boundaries in his or her own life can be drawn to boundary-busters and see them as "normal."

2. What freedoms come in relationships with boundary-lovers?

BOUNDARY BUILDING ————————

In the past, how have you responded to people who can say a clear no? How do you respond now? How do you want to respond? Who are the boundary-lovers in your life? If your list is short, where will you go to find some boundary-lovers?

Measurement #3: Joining the family

1. Explain why it is critical to join the "boundaried family" and have supportive relationships as you develop and strengthen your boundaries. Consider Jesus' words in Matthew 18:20.

2. Where can you go to find supportive, safe relationships?

BOUNDARY BUILDING —————

When has the friendship of someone with similar biblical values helped you stand strong? Be specific. How could (or does) being part of a boundaried family help you with your boundaries?

Measurement #4: Treasuring our treasures

1. What are some of the consequences of taking responsibility for anyone other than yourself?

2. Why is it important and biblical to value ourselves and treasure our treasures? Answer this question in terms of biblical stewardship and responsibility.

BOUNDARY BUILDING —————

Scripture teaches that "we love because [God] first loved us" (1 John 4:19). In other words, we learn to be loving because we are loved. What did you learn about your worth, your lovableness, as a child? As a result of those childhood lessons, how well do you take care of yourself—your feelings, talents, thoughts, attitudes, behavior, body, and the resources God has entrusted to you? Support this answer with details from your life. Begin a list of your "treasures"— your time, money, feelings, and beliefs. How do you want others to treat them? How do you want others to *not* treat them?

Measurement #5: Practicing baby no's

1 What are some effective ways of saying no or telling the truth? Come up with responses for the following situations:

• A church acquaintance asks you to serve on yet another committee

- A good friend needs to talk right now, just as you started the promised reading time with your young child

- Your neighbor asks for your honest opinion about a new (and disastrous) haircut

- Your irresponsible coworker asks you to take on some additional work which will enable him or her to complete a report assigned long ago and due tomorrow

- Your accountant suggests that you fudge on your taxes or a coworker encourages you to be less than honest on your expense report

2. In what current real-life situation do you need to say no or be a truth-teller? Choose the words and practice saying them now.

BOUNDARY BUILDING —————

What past injuries make setting limits and saying no difficult for you? With whom can you practice saying no (Prov. 10:18; Lev. 19:17)? What support group and/or good friend(s) will you ask if you could work on boundaries with them? When will you make that request?

Measurement #6: Rejoicing in the guilty feelings

1. Why do people who are starting to set boundaries often feel guilt and self-condemnation—and why is that feeling a good sign?

2. What is the source of an overactive but inaccurate conscience, with its guilt-inducing "how could you?" messages? What steps can a person take to silence that enslaving voice?

BOUNDARY BUILDING ————

What evidence is there that you have an overactive and unbiblically harsh internal judge? Give specific examples of the kind of condemning self-talk that goes on in your mind or refer to people who have helped you recognize that critical internal voice for what it is. In what boundary setting will you feel like you are transgressing when you aren't? What are you going to do with that guilt?

REVIEWING BOUNDARY MEASUREMENTS

- Resentment is our_____signal, making us aware that someone is violating our boundaries.

- A change of_____indicates that we are attracted to, rather than put off by, boundary-lovers.

- Joining the boundaried_____provides us a safe place to practice our no's and maintain our boundaries.

- When we begin treasuring our_____, we can see that we are letting ourselves receive the love we need in order to begin loving ourselves and others in a freer, more biblical way.

- We start practicing_____ _____when we feel supported and therefore ready to communicate our new boundaries.

- Then, as we communicate those limits and say those no's, we feel_____and we rejoice in those feelings, celebrating the growth and the freedom from unbiblical restraints that the guilt indicates.

SUGGESTED READING ———————

For more thoughts on this session's topic, read the first half of chapter 15 in *Boundaries*: "How to Measure Success with Boundaries." For a more thorough self-evaluation, look at the first part of chapter 13 in the *Boundaries Workbook.*

Boundary Successes, Part II

OVERVIEW

In this session you will

- Look briefly at the five remaining measurable indications of growth toward healthy boundaries

- Reflect on where you are in your development of boundaries

VIDEO SEGMENT
Success with Boundaries

- *Measurement #7: Practicing grown-up no's.* There comes a time when you need to deal with the extremely complicated and even frightening relationships and situations in your life and practice grown-up no's. You need to deal with your number one "boundary buster" and the people in your life with whom it's difficult to set limits. Straightening out these relationships is a major goal in becoming a boundaried person. Setting important limits with such significant people and in significant circumstances involving key issues in life is the fruit of much work and maturing. And our real target is maturity: the ability to love successfully and work successfully, the goal of having a character structure that has boundaries and that can set limits on self and others at the appropriate times, the goal of becoming more like Christ.

- *Measurement #8: Rejoicing in the absence of guilty feelings.* With consistent work and good support, the guilt we are to rejoice in eventually diminishes. That point comes when we have shifted from listening to our overactive conscience and respond instead according to the biblical values of love, responsibility, and forgiveness. These values will have been reinforced by many, many experiences with loving, truthful people who understand boundaries.

- *Measurement #9: Loving the boundaries of others.* If we expect others to respect our boundaries, we need to respect theirs. First, when we are concerned about protecting the treasures of others, we work against the self-centeredness that is part of our fallen nature. Second, loving others' boundaries increases our capacity to care about others. It isn't difficult to love the agreeable parts of people. It's another story, however, when we encounter resistance, confrontation, or separateness. Loving others stretches those muscles.

- *Measurement #10: Freeing our no and our yes.* Learn not to promise too much before you have done your spiritual and emotional calculations. When you're not sure about something, say no. It is more responsible to give out of our resources than to promise that which we might not be able to deliver. And freeing your no like that also frees your yes. When you can say no without conflict, you can freely— without resentment and not being motivated by guilt—say yes to love and service.

- *Measurement #11: Value-driven goal setting.* The ultimate goal of learning boundaries is to free us up to protect, nurture, and develop the lives God has given us stewardship over. Individuals with mature boundaries have a direction in their lives. They make choices based not on the fear of other people's reactions, but based instead on what they have worked out under God to be important for their life. Their goals are not based on emotion but values. They plan ahead, understanding and allowing for resistance to boundaries and goals and ultimately experiencing the joy of desires fulfilled. People with mature limits know that, should it be needed, a no is waiting inside the heart to be used to protect and develop the time, talents, and treasures that God has allocated to them.

LET'S TALK
Success with Boundaries

Directions

1. Split into groups of four or five.

2. In your group, discuss the first question for each measurement found below.

3. A second question is provided if time allows.

4. You will have 15 minutes to complete this exercise.

Measurement #7: Practicing grown-up no's

1. According to 1 John 3:2 ("Dear friends, now we are children of God, and what we will be has not yet been made known. But we know that when he appears, we shall be like him, for we shall see him as he is"), what is the ultimate goal of boundary work? Why are grown-up no's essential to reaching that goal?

2. Why should a person practicing grown-up no's have some support?

BOUNDARY BUILDING ————————

Who is your number-one "boundary buster"? Who else makes the list of boundary busters in your life? What specific treasures are being violated in your relationships with these people? What specific boundaries do you need to set to protect those treasures?

Measurement #8: Rejoicing in the absence of guilty feelings

1. What kinds of experiences can help quiet the voice of a harsh internal parent?

2. Are you noticing an easing up of guilty feelings and an increase of empathic sorrow? Point to a specific instance of setting limits which might have caused you greater guilt and more self-recriminations had it happened a while back.

BOUNDARY BUILDING ————————

Identify some of the people God has placed in your life and some of the situations he has seen you through which have helped quiet your harsh internal parent.

Measurement #9: Loving the boundaries of others

1. We are commanded to love our neighbors as ourselves (Gal. 5:14). What does this command mean when it comes to other people's boundaries?

2. Before people start setting boundaries, how do they tend to respond to the boundaries of others? Why?

BOUNDARY BUILDING —————

How do you tend to respond to others' boundaries? How would you like to respond to their boundaries?

Measurement #10: Freeing our no and our yes

1. Why does freeing our no also free our yes?

2. What often happens when people say yes out of guilt or compliance? How do they feel if they live out their yes?

BOUNDARY BUILDING ———————

What do you plan to do the next time someone asks you for something you aren't sure you can give?

Measurement #11: Value-driven goal setting

1. What impact do boundaries—or a lack of them—have on the pace of life?

2. Explain why healthy, godly boundaries are a matter of good stewardship of the life with which God has gifted us. Why do mature and wise boundaries bear the joyful fruit of desires fulfilled?

BOUNDARY BUILDING ———————

Does your life tend toward a frantic or a steady pace? Does life feel in a hurry or out of control, or do you feel as if you're making steady progress toward a goal? How do your boundaries—or lack of them—contribute to the state of your life? What are you doing to stand strong against resistance to boundaries? What weapons do you now have in your arsenal?

VIDEO SEGMENT
Sherrie with Boundaries

- Remember Sherrie from Session #1? She stumbled through the day in a haphazard, out-of-control fashion. But Sherrie has restructured her life, adding boundaries, setting limits, and living within those.

- Sherrie's day is now characterized by the freedom, self-control, and intimacy that result from a lifestyle based on a godly understanding of boundaries.

- Sherrie's example is not a fairy-tale fantasy. It's a real-life experience that you yourself can experience or perhaps already are experiencing. Like Sherrie, you can learn to take ownership of your life. You can learn what things are your responsibility and what aren't. You can stop taking on problems that God never intended you to take on. You can learn to live by biblical boundaries and experience the relationships and achieve the purposes that God intends for you.

THE BENEFITS OF HEALTHY BOUNDARIES

- Healthier_____patterns

- A better relationship with_____ _____

- A diet and_____program that works for you

- The perspective that dieting and exercise is good_____
  _____, not selfishness

- More effective_____skills: bedtimes for the
  children; shared household tasks; letting them be responsible for getting to the carpool ride on time

- Greater effectiveness at_____: punctuality; respect;
  recognition

- More honest_____ _____

- _____family time

- A more fulfilling and joy-filled_____: parenting
  together; setting limits with your spouse and standing by
  clearly defined consequences; being more of a team with a
  new sense of mutual love and mutual responsibility; being
  unafraid of conflict, forgiving of each other's mistakes,
  respectful of each other's boundaries

- Clear limits on and wiser choices with_____
  commitments

- A stronger relationship with_____

- A solid_____ group

ON YOUR OWN
Boundary Building

Directions

On your own, take 10 minutes to reflect on and answer the following questions.

1. Consider the areas listed on page 119. Where have you seen progress in your own life? Take time to thank God for that progress.

2. In which of the areas listed do you still have work to do? What boundary work are you doing in those areas? Be specific about your plan and your current efforts in regard to those issues.

SUGGESTED READING ——————

For more thoughts on this session's topic, read the second half of chapter 15 in *Boundaries:* "How to Measure Success with Boundaries." For a more thorough self-evaluation, look at the second part of chapter 13 in the *Boundaries*

For information on books, resources or speaking engagements:

Cloud-Townsend Resources
3176 Pullman Avenue, Suite 104
Costa Mesa, CA 92626
Phone: 1-800-676-HOPE (4673)
Web: www.cloudtownsend.com

About the Writer

Lisa Guest writes, edits, and develops curriculum from her home in Irvine, California, where she lives with her husband and two children. She has written two books, *Small Miracles* and *A Mother's Love.* She enjoys swimming, reading, and playing with her kids.

Boundaries

This book presents a biblical treatment of boundaries, identifies how boundaries are developed, and how they become injured, shows Christian misconceptions of their function and purpose, and gives a program for developing and maintaining healthy limits.

Hardcover 0-310-58590-2

Audio pages 0-310-58598-8

The Best of Boundaries—Video

Finally, some help for Christians who are overworked, overwrought, and overcommitted. This thirty-minute highlight video gives a brief overview of the eight-session *Boundaries* video course.

0-310-24589-3

Boundaries with Kids

This book helps parents set boundaries with their children and helps them teach the concept of boundaries to their children.

Hardcover 0-310-20035-0

Audio pages 0-310-20456-9

Workbook 0-310-22349-0

Changes That Heal
Dr. Henry Cloud

This book focuses on four developmental tasks—bonding to others, separating from others, integrating good and bad in our lives, and taking charge of our lives—that all of us must accomplish to heal our inner pain and to enable us to function and grow emotionally and spiritually. The condensed audio version of the book is read by the author.

Softcover 0-310-60631-4

Mass market 0-310-21463-7

Audio Pages® Abridged Cassettes 0-310-20567-0

Workbook 0-310-60633-0

Hiding from Love
Dr. John Townsend

Help for identifying and healing from harmful withdrawal behavior and creating healthy, fulfilling relationships.

Softcover 0-310-20107-1

The Mom Factor

Drs. Henry Cloud and John Townsend identify six types of moms and show how they profoundly affect our lives.

Hardcover 0-310-20036-9

Softcover 0-310-22559-0

Audio pages 0-310-20453-4

Workbook 0-310-21533-1

Safe People

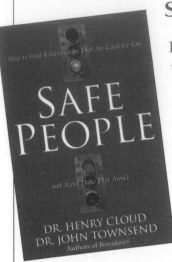

Finding safe people provides the foundation for building healthy, lasting relationships. Here's how to identify safe people in your life.

Hardcover 0-310-59560-6

Softcover 0-310-21084-4

Audio Pages® Abridged Cassettes 0-310-59568-1

Audio Pages® Unabridged Cassettes 0-310-24560-5

Workbook 0-310-49501-6

Twelve "Christian" Beliefs That Can Drive You Crazy

This workbook format helps people understand twelve common but false assumptions that cripple their faith.

Softcover 0-310-49491-5

ZONDERVAN™

GRAND RAPIDS, MICHIGAN 49530

www.zondervan.com

We want to hear from you. Please send your comments about this
book to us in care of the address below. Thank you.

GRAND RAPIDS, MICHIGAN 49530

www.zondervan.com